soups

Gooseberry Patch

Classics

Soup is a lot like a family.
Each ingredient enhances the others.
– Marge Kennedy

French Onion Soup with Gruyére

4 T. butter
4 sweet onions, thinly sliced
1/4 c. sugar
salt and pepper to taste

3 16-oz. cans beef
  broth, divided
Optional: 2 T. cooking sherry
4 slices rye bread, toasted
1 c. Gruyére cheese, grated

Melt butter in a stockpot over low heat; add onions. Heat, covered, until onions are soft, about 20 minutes; stir occasionally. Sprinkle sugar on top; increase heat, stirring onions until caramelized. Reduce heat; salt and pepper to taste. Pour in 1-1/2 cans beef broth; simmer, uncovered, for 15 minutes. Add remaining broth and sherry, if desired; simmer for 35 minutes. Set 4 oven-proof bowls on a baking sheet; fill with onion mixture. Add a slice of rye toast to each bowl; sprinkle cheese on top. Broil until cheese melts. Serves 4.

Parmesan-Onion Soup

4 c. onion, thinly sliced
3 T. butter, melted
1/2 t. sugar
1 T. all-purpose flour
4 c. water

salt and pepper to taste
4 French bread slices,
  toasted
1/2 c. grated Parmesan
  cheese

Sauté onion in butter until tender in a stockpot; stir in sugar and flour until dissolved, about 3 to 5 minutes. Add water; simmer, covered, for 30 minutes. Season with salt and pepper. Fill 4 oven-proof bowls with soup; top with a bread slice. Sprinkle with Parmesan cheese. Bake at 400 degrees until cheese melts. Serves 4.

Wild Rice Soup

1 c. wild rice
3 c. chicken broth
1-lb. pkg. sliced bacon,
    crisply cooked and
    crumbled, drippings
    reserved
1 onion, chopped

2 10-3/4 oz. cans cream of
    potato soup
2 4-oz. cans sliced
    mushrooms, undrained
2 c. half-and-half
5-oz. jar sharp pasteurized
    process cheese spread
2 c. water

Simmer rice in chicken broth until all liquid is absorbed; set aside. Spoon bacon drippings into a saucepan; sauté onion until tender. Stir in bacon, cream of potato soup, mushrooms, half-and-half, cheese, water and rice; warm through without boiling. Makes 12 cups.

Make a new neighbor feel welcome by giving a loaf of homemade bread on a cutting board, a set of soup bowls and a favorite soup recipe. How thoughtful!

Velvet Tomato Soup

2 T. unsalted butter
1 onion, coarsely chopped
1 clove garlic, minced
2 T. fresh tarragon leaves,
    chopped
1/2 t. allspice
1/2 t. sugar
6 c. chicken broth

3 lbs. plum tomatoes, peeled
    and coarsely chopped
1 T. tomato paste
1 T. orange zest
1 c. whipping cream
Garnish: 2 T. fresh chives,
    chopped

Melt butter in a heavy stockpot over medium-low heat; sauté
onion until tender, about 10 minutes. Stir in garlic, tarragon,
allspice and sugar; stir for one minute. Pour in chicken broth,
tomatoes and tomato paste; bring to a boil. Reduce heat; cover
and simmer for 30 minutes. Remove from heat; stir in orange
zest and set aside to cool to room temperature. Purée soup in
batches until smooth; return to stockpot. Stir in cream over low
heat; heat until warmed without boiling. Ladle into bowls;
garnish with chives. Makes 6 to 8 servings.

Just for fun, spear a cherry
tomato or a chunk of
Cheddar cheese with a
toothpick and use as
a garnish.

Chicken Noodle Soup

2 6-oz. cans chicken
2 cubes chicken bouillon
4 c. water
3-oz. pkg. creamy chicken
   ramen noodles with
   seasoning packet,
   divided
1 t. poultry seasoning

1 T. fresh parsley, chopped
1 c. milk
4 carrots, chopped
4 stalks celery, chopped
1 c. frozen peas
1 c. frozen corn
1/2 onion, chopped

Place chicken, bouillon and water in a 4-cup measuring cup; microwave on high for 5 minutes. Add ramen noodle seasoning packet, poultry seasoning, parsley and milk; stir. Pour chicken mixture and vegetables into a Dutch oven; boil for 5 to 7 minutes. Break ramen noodles in half and add. Boil for an additional 3 to 4 minutes. Reduce heat and serve within 5 minutes. Makes 6 to 8 servings.

Invite friends over for a Soup Supper during a frosty winter afternoon or evening. Ask everyone to bring their favorite soup or bread to share...you provide the bowls, spoons and a crackling fire!

Baked Potato Soup

6 potatoes
1/3 c. butter
1/3 c. all-purpose flour
4 c. milk

1 c. sour cream
Garnish: shredded Cheddar
   cheese, chopped green
   onions and bacon bits

Pierce potatoes with a fork; microwave on high for 10 minutes, turn and microwave until soft, about 10 minutes. Peel and cube; mash half the potatoes and set aside. Whisk butter and flour together in a saucepan over low heat until smooth and thick; add milk, whisking until thickened. Heat over medium heat for 5 to 10 more minutes. Add potatoes, both mashed and cubed; stir in sour cream. Heat thoroughly without boiling. Spoon into serving bowls; garnish with toppings. Makes 4 to 6 servings.

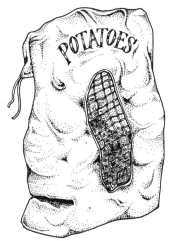

Spice up Baked Potato Soup with crushed tortilla chips,
shredded Pepper Jack cheese and chopped
jalapeño peppers.

Cheeseburger Soup

3/4 c. onion, chopped
3/4 c. carrots, shredded
3/4 c. celery, diced
1 t. dried basil
1 t. dried parsley
4 T. butter, divided
3 c. chicken broth
4 c. potatoes, peeled and
  diced

1/2 lb. ground beef, browned
1/4 c. all-purpose flour
2 c. pasteurized process
  cheese spread, cubed
1-1/2 c. milk
3/4 t. salt
1/4 t. pepper
1/4 c. sour cream

Sauté onion, carrots, celery, basil and parsley in one tablespoon butter until vegetables are tender, 10 minutes; add broth, potatoes and beef. Bring soup to a boil; reduce heat, cover and simmer for 10 to 12 minutes or until potatoes are tender. Melt remaining butter in a small skillet; whisk in flour until bubbly, about 3 to 5 minutes. Add flour mixture to soup; bring to a boil. Heat and stir for 2 minutes; reduce heat to low. Add cheese, milk, salt and pepper; stir until cheese melts. Remove from heat and blend in sour cream; serve warm. Serves 4.

Did you know...?
You can drop a few
lettuce leaves into a
pot of soup to absorb
any excess grease.

Farmhouse Beef Stew

3 lbs. beef stew, cubed
2 T. shortening
2 onions, sliced
2 cloves garlic, minced
1 c. celery, chopped
1/4 c. fresh parsley, chopped
2-1/2 c. tomatoes, chopped
1/2 t. dried thyme

1 T. salt
pepper to taste
3-1/4 c. water, divided
1 c. peas
12 carrots, sliced
2 onions, chopped
6 potatoes, cubed
1/2 c. all-purpose flour

Brown meat in shortening in a Dutch oven; stir in the next
8 ingredients and 2-1/2 cups water. Bring to a boil; reduce heat
and simmer for 2 hours. Add peas, carrots, onions and
potatoes; simmer for one hour. Whisk flour into remaining
water until smooth; stir into stew. Simmer for 5 minutes.
Makes 6 servings.

Fresh garden vegetables make the best broth and it's
so easy to make! Just add chopped carrots, onions or
cabbage to a pot of boiling water and simmer 30 minutes.
Cool and then freeze in ice cube trays until ready to use.

Smoked Sausage Stew

1-1/4 lbs. smoked sausage, sliced
15-oz. can French onion soup
6-oz. can whole tomatoes, undrained
2 c. potatoes, cubed
1/2 t. Worcestershire sauce
15-1/4 oz. can corn, drained and liquid reserved
1/4 c. all-purpose flour

Brown sausage in a Dutch oven; drain. Add onion soup, tomatoes, potatoes, Worcestershire sauce and corn; bring to a boil. Reduce heat and simmer for 20 minutes or until potatoes are tender. Whisk 1/2 cup reserved corn liquid into flour; gradually add to sausage mixture. Heat over medium heat, stirring constantly, until thick. Makes 4 to 6 servings.

Cowboy Stew

5 to 6 potatoes, peeled and cubed
2 carrots, peeled and sliced
1 lb. ground beef
1 T. all-purpose flour
8-oz. can tomato sauce

Boil potatoes and carrots in a saucepan until tender, about 30 minutes; set aside. Shape beef into one-inch meatballs; brown in a skillet and drain. Pour meatballs into undrained vegetable mixture; heat for 5 minutes and set aside. Whisk flour with 1/2 cup water; add tomato sauce. Stir into beef mixture; cover and simmer for 15 minutes. Serves 4.

Williamsburg Turkey Soup

2 onions, chopped
3 stalks celery, chopped
2 carrots, chopped
2 c. water
1 c. butter
1 c. all-purpose flour

2-1/2 qts. turkey or chicken
   broth
1 pt. half-and-half
1 c. turkey, cooked and
   chopped
1 c. prepared rice
salt and pepper to taste

Combine onions, celery, carrots and water in a medium
saucepan; heat over medium heat for 20 minutes. Melt butter
over low heat in a Dutch oven; whisk in flour until smooth.
Whisk in broth and half-and-half until bubbly, about 4 to
5 minutes; add undrained vegetables. Heat for 10 minutes,
stirring occasionally; add remaining ingredients, heating
thoroughly. Serves 10 to 12.

Warm up the soup tureen
before pouring in homemade
soup and it'll stay hot longer.
Just fill with hot water, let
sit for a few minutes, pour
out the water and
it's ready!

Chicken Gumbo

4 slices bacon, crisply
   cooked and crumbled
1 c. onion, chopped
1 c. green pepper, chopped
1 c. celery, chopped
1 clove garlic, minced
6 boneless, skinless chicken
   breasts, cooked and
   chopped

4 14-1/2 oz. cans chicken
   broth
2 t. salt
1/4 t. pepper
15-oz. can tomato and
   herb sauce
16-oz. pkg. frozen, sliced
   okra

Place bacon, onion, green pepper, celery and garlic in a Dutch oven; sauté for 3 minutes. Add chicken, chicken broth, salt and pepper; simmer, covered, for 30 minutes. Stir in tomato sauce and okra; simmer until okra is tender, about 30 minutes. Makes 8 to 10 servings.

For a really quick side dish, cook chopped green peppers in butter for about 5 minutes. Add canned corn and salt and simmer until warmed through...yummy.

Italian Wedding Soup

1 lb. ground beef
1 lb. ground sausage
4 eggs, divided
1 c. bread crumbs
2 t. dried oregano
1 t. dried rosemary
1 clove garlic, minced
olive oil

2 15-oz. cans chicken broth
5-oz. pkg. vermicelli
1 c. spinach leaves, torn
1 onion, diced
6 mushrooms, thinly sliced
Garnish: grated Parmesan
    cheese

Combine beef, sausage, 2 eggs, bread crumbs, oregano, rosemary and garlic together; shape into one-inch meatballs. Brown in olive oil; drain and set aside. Bring broth and 2 canfuls water to a boil in a heavy stockpot; add meatballs, vermicelli and spinach. Reduce heat; simmer, uncovered, until pasta is soft. Stir in onion and mushrooms. Lightly beat remaining eggs; drop into soup, stirring until cooked. Remove soup from heat; spoon into serving bowls. Garnish with Parmesan cheese. Serves 10.

Making meatballs from scratch? Instead of baking, cook 'em quick by just dropping into boiling water. They'll be lower in fat and will keep their shape too! Boil for a few minutes and meatballs will be ready to go into sauces or into the freezer for another day.

Golden Summer Soup

1 onion, chopped
2 T. oil
2 to 3 roma tomatoes,
   chopped
1-1/2 lbs. yellow squash,
   chopped

3 c. chicken broth
1 c. buttermilk
1/4 c. fresh basil, chopped
Garnish: roma tomatoes,
   sliced and fresh basil

Sauté onion in oil in a stockpot over medium heat until golden, about 10 minutes; add tomatoes, stirring until soft. Stir in squash and chicken broth; bring to a boil over high heat. Reduce heat; simmer, covered, until squash is tender, about 20 minutes. Purée mixture with buttermilk in a blender until smooth; stir in basil. Serve warm or cold; garnish with tomato slice and additional basil before serving. Makes 8 servings.

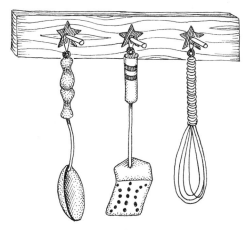

Keep tomatoes stem side down and out of the fridge for fresh-from-the-garden taste.

Smoky Pumpkin Soup

6 c. pumpkin, peeled and
   chopped
6 slices bacon, crisply cooked
   and crumbled, drippings
   reserved
4 T. butter
6 c. beef broth

1/2 c. Marsala wine or
   beef broth
1 t. dried thyme
salt and pepper to taste
Garnish: roasted pumpkin
   seeds

Sauté pumpkin in a stockpot in reserved bacon drippings and butter for 15 minutes, stirring occasionally; add broth. Reduce heat and simmer, covered, until pumpkin is tender, about 30 minutes; remove from heat. Add wine or broth, thyme, salt and pepper; purée in batches until smooth. Return to stockpot; add bacon. Simmer for about 10 minutes. Serve immediately sprinkled with pumpkin seeds. Makes 6 servings.

Get the whole family together on a sunny Autumn day and take a hayride at a local pumpkin patch! After the fun, warm up with some homemade soup.

Red Pepper Soup

6 red peppers, chopped
2 carrots, chopped
2 onions, chopped
1 stalk celery, chopped
4 cloves garlic, minced
1 T. olive oil
64-oz. can chicken broth

1/2 c. long-grain rice,
    uncooked
2 t. dried thyme
1-1/2 t. salt
1/4 t. pepper
1/4 t. cayenne pepper
1/8 t. crushed red pepper
    flakes

Sauté red peppers, carrots, onions, celery and garlic in olive oil in a Dutch oven until tender; add remaining ingredients. Bring to a boil; reduce heat and simmer, covered, for 20 to 25 minutes. Remove from heat; cool for 30 minutes. Purée in small batches; return to Dutch oven and warm thoroughly. Makes 8 servings.

Freeze summer vegetables to enjoy year 'round! Combine them in gallon-size plastic zipping bags...hearty stews and soups will be ready in no time.

Cream of Garlic Soup

3/4 lb. cooked ham, cubed
1 onion, chopped
10 cloves garlic, halved
2 potatoes, peeled and cubed
2 T. butter

1/4 c. oil
6 c. chicken broth
1 c. whipping cream
1 c. half-and-half
salt and pepper to taste

Sauté ham, onion, garlic and potatoes together in a 10" skillet with butter and oil until onion is tender. Pour into a stockpot; add chicken broth. Simmer for one hour; remove from heat. Purée in batches in a blender; return mixture to stockpot. Whisk in whipping cream and half-and-half; heat through without boiling. Season with salt and pepper. Serves 6.

Save the water that the potatoes were
boiled in...add to soups and sauces to
thicken and add flavor.

New England Cheddar Cheese Soup

1 green pepper, diced
1 carrot, diced
1 onion, diced
1 stalk celery, diced
6 T. butter, divided
1/2 c. all-purpose flour

2-1/2 qts. warm milk
1-1/4 c. chicken broth
3/4 c. shredded Cheddar
   cheese
1 c. shredded American
   cheese

Sauté green pepper, carrot, onion and celery in 3 tablespoons butter in a 12" skillet until tender, about 10 minutes; remove vegetables to a bowl. Add remaining butter to same skillet; whisk in flour until smooth. Remove from heat; whisk in milk and broth. Return to heat; stir until thickened, about 10 minutes. Add vegetables; heat through. Reduce heat to low; stir in cheeses until melted. Serves 8 to 10.

Try this soup with shredded sharp Cheddar cheese for extra bite or mix in 1/4 cup mozzarella or Monterey Jack cheese for an even creamier soup.

★ Classics ★

Sausage Soup

4-oz. pkg. hot Italian
  sausage links, thickly
  sliced
4-oz. pkg. sweet Italian
  sausage links, thickly
  sliced
1/2 c. onion, chopped
2 potatoes, peeled and
  chopped

2 14-1/2 oz. cans chicken
  broth
10-oz. pkg. frozen chopped
  spinach
1/2 c. water
1/4 t. pepper

Brown sausages and onion in a heavy stockpot; drain. Add
remaining ingredients; bring to a boil. Reduce heat; simmer,
covered, until potatoes are tender, about 20 minutes. Makes
6 servings.

Creole Soup

2 28-oz. cans diced
  tomatoes
28-oz. can crushed tomatoes
3 10-3/4 oz. cans beef broth
2 c. green pepper, diced

2 c. onion, chopped
2 c. celery, chopped
1/4 c. wine vinegar
1 t. prepared horseradish
2 c. elbow macaroni, cooked

Place tomatoes, broth, one can water, green pepper, onion,
celery, vinegar and horseradish in a stockpot. Simmer for
10 minutes; add macaroni and continue to simmer until
warmed through. Makes 10 to 12 servings.

Beef & Black-Eyed Pea Soup

2 lbs. ground beef
1/2 c. green pepper, chopped
1/2 c. butter
1/2 c. all-purpose flour
2 qts. water
28-oz. can chopped tomatoes
16-oz. pkg. frozen black-
  eyed peas
1 c. onion, chopped
1 c. carrots, diced
1 c. celery, chopped
2 T. beef bouillon granules
1 T. pepper
1/2 t. salt
1/4 t. garlic powder
1/4 t. onion powder
1-1/2 c. prepared rice

Brown beef and green pepper in a skillet; drain. Melt butter in a
Dutch oven; add flour, whisking until smooth. Cook one
minute, stirring constantly. Gradually add water; stir until
bubbly. Stir in beef mixture and all remaining ingredients,
except rice. Bring to a boil; cover and simmer 45 minutes to
one hour. Add rice during last 15 minutes. Serves 6 to 8.

Cooked beans add extra flavor to hearty soups and
stews. Just mash and freeze in an ice cube tray. Store
them in freezer bags then just toss into the pot!

Creamy Onion-Potato Soup

3 T. butter	1/4 t. pepper
5 c. onions, chopped	1/2 t. celery seed
6 c. potatoes, cubed	2-1/2 t. garlic salt
4 c. vegetable broth	3 c. milk
3 cloves garlic, chopped	1 carrot, grated

Melt butter in a 4-quart saucepan; sauté onions until soft. Add potatoes, vegetable broth, garlic, pepper, celery seed and garlic salt; bring to a boil. Reduce heat and simmer, covered, for 20 to 30 minutes or until potatoes are tender. Cool slightly and, working with small portions at a time, purée in a blender. Return to stockpot; add milk. Heat until warmed but do not boil; stir in carrot before serving. Serves 6.

Give favorite homemade soups extra flavor by substituting one cup of stock for one cup of milk in the recipe.

Garden Vegetable Soup

2/3 c. carrot, sliced
1/2 c. onion, diced
2 cloves garlic, minced
3 c. vegetable broth

1-1/2 c. cabbage, chopped
1/2 c. frozen green beans
1 T. catsup
1 T. Italian seasoning

Sauté carrot, onion and garlic for 5 minutes in a stockpot sprayed with non-stick vegetable spray; add remaining ingredients. Bring to a boil; reduce heat and simmer, covered, for 15 minutes or until beans are tender. Makes 4 servings.

Corn Chowder

1 onion, chopped
2 T. butter
2 c. potatoes, diced
1 c. hot water
2 T. all-purpose flour

2 c. milk
10-oz. pkg. frozen corn
1 t. salt
1/8 t. pepper

Sauté onion in butter in a stockpot until golden; add potatoes and water. Bring to a boil; reduce heat and simmer, covered, until potatoes are tender, about 20 minutes. Gradually whisk flour into milk; pour into the stockpot. Add remaining ingredients; bring to a boil. Reduce heat; simmer for 10 minutes, stirring occasionally. Serves 4.

Fireside Chili

1-1/2 lbs. ground beef or
    pork
1 c. green pepper, chopped
1 c. onion, chopped
2 15-oz. cans red kidney
    beans, drained
28-oz. can tomatoes,
    chopped and undrained
15-oz. can tomato sauce

1-1/2 c. water
2 T. chili powder
2 T. Worcestershire sauce
1 T. honey
1 t. salt
1/2 t. dried basil
1/2 t. cinnamon
1/4 t. allspice
1 bay leaf

In a 4-quart Dutch oven, sauté meat with green pepper and onion until meat is browned and vegetables are tender; drain. Add kidney beans, tomatoes, tomato sauce, water, chili powder, Worcestershire sauce, honey, salt, basil, cinnamon, allspice and bay leaf. Simmer, uncovered, for 30 minutes; cover and simmer for one hour, stirring occasionally. Serves 6 to 8.

Wrap up a big pot of Fireside Chili and deliver it to a friend who's feeling under the weather...how thoughtful!

The Ultimate White Chili

1 T. oil
1 lb. boneless, skinless
    chicken breasts, chopped
1/2 c. shallots, chopped
3 cloves garlic, minced
14-1/2 oz. can whole
    tomatoes, coarsely
    chopped
14-1/2 oz. can chicken broth
11-oz. can tomatillos,
    drained and chopped

4-1/2 oz. can green chilies,
    chopped
1/2 t. dried oregano
1/2 t. coriander seed,
    crushed
1/4 t. cumin
2 16-oz. cans Great
    Northern beans, drained
3 T. lime juice
1/4 t. pepper
1 c. Pepper Jack cheese,
    shredded

Spray a stockpot with non-stick cooking spray; add oil and
heat over medium-high heat until hot. Sauté chicken for
3 minutes or until juices run clear when pierced with a fork.
Remove chicken; set aside. Add shallots and garlic to same
stockpot; sauté 2 minutes or until tender. Stir in tomatoes and
next 6 ingredients. Bring to a boil; reduce heat and simmer for
20 minutes. Add chicken and beans; heat thoroughly. Stir in
lime juice and pepper. Ladle into bowls; sprinkle with cheese.
Serves 6.

Farmstead Split Pea Soup

8 c. water
1-lb. pkg. split peas, rinsed
  and drained
1 ham bone with meat
2 onions, chopped
3 leeks, white part only,
  chopped
2 stalks celery, chopped

1 carrot, peeled and chopped
1 c. dry white wine or
  chicken broth
1 clove garlic, minced
1/2 t. dried marjoram
1/4 t. dried thyme
salt and pepper to taste

Combine all ingredients in a Dutch oven except for the salt and pepper. Bring to a boil; reduce heat, cover and simmer for 2 to 2-1/2 hours or until peas are soft. Remove ham bone and cool soup to warm. Remove meat from bone; add meat to Dutch oven. Salt and pepper to taste. Makes 8 servings.

Herbs from your garden will look (and smell!) wonderful hanging from peg boards or windowsills. Hang several bundles in the kitchen for adding snips to favorite soups and stews.

Apple-Barley Soup

2 onions, thinly sliced
2 T. oil
3-1/2 c. vegetable broth
1-1/2 c. apple cider
1/3 c. pearled barley
2 carrots, diced
1 t. dried thyme

1/4 t. dried marjoram
1 bay leaf
2 c. apples, cored, peeled
   and chopped
1/4 c. fresh parsley, minced
1 T. lemon juice
1/4 t. salt

Sauté onions in oil over medium heat in a stockpot until tender; reduce heat. Cover and simmer for 10 minutes, stirring occasionally, until caramelized. Add broth, cider, barley, carrots, thyme, marjoram and bay leaf; cover and simmer for one hour or until barley is tender. Combine remaining ingredients in a small bowl; add to soup and simmer for 5 minutes or until apples are tender. Discard bay leaf before serving. Makes 4 to 6 servings.

You're the apple of my eye!

Too much salt in the soup? Just slice a potato in half and drop it into the pot...remove before serving for a perfect pot of soup.

Crabmeat Soup

1 cube vegetable bouillon
1 c. boiling water
1/4 c. onion, chopped
1/4 c. margarine
2 T. all-purpose flour
1 t. salt
1/4 t. celery salt
1/8 t. pepper
1 t. hot pepper sauce
2 c. milk
2 c. half-and-half
1 lb. flaked crabmeat
Garnish: fresh parsley, chopped

Dissolve bouillon in water; set aside. Sauté onion in margarine until tender; whisk in flour and seasonings. Gradually pour in milk, half-and-half and bouillon mixture; stir until thickened. Stir in crabmeat; heat until warmed without boiling. Spoon into serving bowls; garnish with parsley. Makes 6 servings.

SEAFOOD
OUR SPECIALTY
fresh catch
DAILY

No crabmeat on hand? Substitute shredded, cooked chicken or even ground turkey for a hearty alternative.

Clam Chowder

1 c. onion, diced	3/4 c. butter
1 c. celery, diced	3/4 c. all-purpose flour
2 c. potatoes, diced	1 qt. half-and-half
2 6-1/2 oz. cans clams,	1-1/2 t. salt
drained and juice	2 T. red wine vinegar
reserved	1/8 t. pepper

Place onion, celery and potatoes in a saucepan; pour clam juice on top. Add just enough water to cover; simmer, covered, over medium heat until tender. Remove from heat; set aside. Melt butter in a 12" skillet; whisk in flour until smooth. Add half-and-half; whisk until thick. Stir in undrained vegetables, clams, salt, vinegar and pepper; warm through without boiling. Serves 4 to 6.

Sourdough bread is traditionally served with Clam Chowder...pick up a ready-made loaf at the grocery and pop it in the oven for a crispy, warm crust!

CATCH OF THE DAY:

MAINE LOBSTER

TRY OUR FRESH CHOWDER

Lemon-Chicken Soup

10 c. chicken broth
3 stalks celery, sliced
3 carrots, sliced
1 onion, chopped
1 c. long-grain rice,
    uncooked

1-1/2 lbs. boneless, skinless
    chicken breasts, cooked
    and chopped
3 eggs, beaten
1/2 c. lemon juice
1 t. dried oregano

Combine broth, celery, carrots and onion in a stockpot; bring to a boil. Add rice and chicken; reduce heat and simmer until rice is tender, about 15 minutes. Combine eggs and lemon juice; gradually add to soup, stirring with a fork until ribbons form. Sprinkle with oregano; simmer for 3 minutes. Serve warm. Makes 8 to 10 servings.

Serving soup as a first course before the main dish?
Allow one cup per guest. When serving
hearty soup as the main dish, allow
2 cups per guest.

Minted Watermelon Soup

1 watermelon, seeded
   and chopped

1-3/4 c. vanilla yogurt
sprigs of fresh mint

Blend enough watermelon to equal 6 cups; add yogurt, blending well. Refrigerate for 2 to 3 hours; spoon into custard cups or fluted glasses. Top with a sprig of fresh mint. Serves 6 to 8.

Strawberry Soup

2 c. fresh whole
   strawberries, hulled and
   divided
1-1/2 c. water, divided
3/4 c. sugar

1 c. cranberry juice
8-oz. carton strawberry
   yogurt
Garnish: fresh mint sprigs

Blend all but 9 strawberries with 1/2 cup water until smooth; pour into a stockpot. Add sugar, remaining water and cranberry juice; bring to a boil. Remove from heat; cool to room temperature. Whisk in yogurt; refrigerate until chilled. Spoon into serving bowls; top with a whole strawberry and sprig of mint. Makes 9 servings.

Roll some fresh grapes, strawberries and mandarin oranges in extra-fine sugar for a glittery (and tasty!) garnish.

from the kitchen of:

Eat Soup

first & eat it
last and live
'til a hundred
years be past.

OLD FRENCH PROVERB

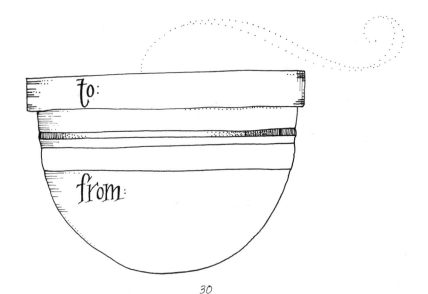

to:

from:

Copy, color and cut
out these little tags
and tie
them on for
extra-special gifts
and surprises.

Thank
You

to:

from:

INDEX

Apple-Barley Soup 25
Baked Potato Soup 6
Beef & Black-Eyed Pea Soup 19
Cheeseburger Soup 7
Chicken Gumbo 11
Chicken Noodle Soup 5
Clam Chowder 27
Corn Chowder 21
Cowboy Stew 9
Crabmeat Soup 26
Cream of Garlic Soup 16
Creamy Onion-Potato Soup 20
Creole Soup 18
Farmhouse Beef Stew 8
Farmstead Split Pea Soup 24
Fireside Chili 22
French Onion Soup with Gruyére 2
Garden Vegetable Soup 21
Golden Summer Soup 13
Italian Wedding Soup 12
Lemon-Chicken Soup 28
Minted Watermelon Soup 29
New England Cheddar Cheese Soup 17
Parmesan-Onion Soup 2
Red Pepper Soup 15
Sausage Soup 18
Smoked Sausage Stew 9
Smoky Pumpkin Soup 14
Strawberry Soup 29
The Ultimate White Chili 23
Velvet Tomato Soup 4
Wild Rice Soup 3
Williamsburg Turkey Soup 10